God Morning

To my dear friend Lori, I love you & appreciate you & all that you give to those you love. Love you! Dr. Barbara A. Cole

By Dr. Barbara Cole

Author: Dr. Barbara Cole
Publication Services–Kingdom News Publication
Services, LLC.

DISCLAIMER
All the material contained in this book is provided for
educational and informational purposes only. No
responsibility can be taken for any results or outcomes
resulting from the use of this material.
While every attempt has been made to provide information
that is both accurate and effective, the author does not
assume any responsibility for the accuracy or use/misuse of
this information.

Printed in the United States of America.
ISBN 978-0998026220

U.S. Copyright Office
101 Independence Ave. S.E.,
Washington, D.C. 20559-6000

KINGDOM NEWS TODAY
Publication Services, LLC

Dedication

I would like to dedicate this book to my wonderful mother, Mary Elizabeth DeClouet Quarles, my very first Prayer partner. Second, I would like to pay a special salute to my eldest brother, Rev. Davis DeClouet, who has joined our mother in the great cloud of witness. Thanks to the both of you who believed in God's word and the power of Prayer.

Acknowledgements

To God, my Heavenly Father. To Jesus Christ my Savior and Redeemer and to His precious Holy Spirit who leads, guides, protects, instructs and comforts me on every level and in every situation.

To my husband Bryan, my soulmate my lover and my best friend. Words can never express my gratitude in how much you love me and how you show the depth of your love for me. Thank you, my handsome and beautiful MG (Man of God) for showing me what true love is all about.

To my beautiful children: Terra, Desralynn and Bryan Adam. I am so very proud of the women and man you have become. Thank you for supporting me through this project. I truly would not have made it without your love, endurance, patience and belief in me that I can do all things through Christ who strengthens me daily. To my son-in-love Dorian who continues to challenge all those around in the importance of expression by use of our words. To my grandsons Branden and Bryson who bring me so much joy.

To my sisters, my big brother who prayed with me, for me and walked with me through one of the most difficult times I've ever encountered.

To my editors, EB and Danika for all the rewrites, corrections and patience through this entire project. I would like to especially thank Angie Alexander for her support and professional skills to help bring this project into fruition. A special thank you to my beautiful daughter-in-love Sarai for your patience, time and talent. Thank you for all your labor of love.

To Kingdom News Publication Services, Ms. Erica McGraw, here's to the next project! Thank you for your trust and belief in me and helping me produce this project for the Kingdom of God and His people.

Reviews

I sensed a flood of God's presence and a longing to beef up my prayer and worship lifestyle through the use of GOD MORNING... Without a doubt, readers can't be casual as they encounter the text as an intentional use to apply prayer and practice of using God's word to address multiple circumstances faced in their daily lives. I can't help but imagine victorious, mature Christians and NEW converts who are investing themselves into Kingdom living. I see translations in many languages coming NEXT. — **EB Brown**

I found this book instructional and spiritual. If you are someone who just doesn't know how or what to pray for or just don't feel worthy. This book will get you through to that point. First in foremost accept who you are and never feel bad for your failures. Keep in mind the spirit is willing, but the flesh is weak. Before you take that final step to pray you must know that you are worthy and that you believe that your prayers are being heard. See yourself accomplishing those things you desire for your life. — **P. Counce**

Excellent job!!! May all who read be blessed, delivered, freed, renewed, touched, changed, healed, and more. By the power of our LORD and Savior Jesus Christ. —**Danika O.**

Introduction
How God Morning Was Birthed

I will lift mine eyes unto the hills, from whence cometh my help. My help comes from the Lord, which made heaven and earth. (Psalm 121:1-2 KJV).

June 8, 2016, was a warm, summer morning in Houston, Texas when I had a heart attack. I will never forget that day; I remembered to call out to the Lord, who did not suffer my foot to be moved. I thank God that He kept me that day. He preserved me from all evil that warm, summer morning. On that day, I called, you answered me, you made me bold and increased my strength (Psalm138:3 NASB). Thank you, God for You gave me courage to reach for the phone to inform my husband that I needed help.

On the previous day, my husband and I had just returned from a speaking engagement in New Orleans, Louisiana. I was home alone, and Bryan was away on his first day of summer school. I, on the other hand, had opted out of teaching that summer. We were both employed as substitute teachers at a school that supported students and their families in special education. I decided not to work summer school because for nearly six months I had been experiencing symptoms that mimicked pneumonia, only to discover I had contracted a H-pylori virus.

Discovering this diagnosis also revealed a very serious heart condition, Left Ventricular Non-Compaction Cardiomyopathy, which led to Congestive Heart Failure (CHF). After a brief stay in the hospital, it was my hope and my faith in the healing virtue of my Lord and Savior that I survived. For in that moment, I knew and understood Hebrews 11:1 (KJV), "Now faith is the substance of things hoped for and the evidence of things not seen." Because of my faith and trust in Him, I am here to share my story and to encourage others to draw closer to Him in those dark and trying times.

Around the fall of 2016 and being new to social media, I decided I wanted to encourage others who may have gone through what I've experienced, since social media could not exist without the powerful use of our words and communities coming together. When I posted on social media for the first time, my opening statement was supposed to be: Good Morning Everyone because He's the one in control of it anyway. What I posted was God Morning instead. When I went to correct it, I felt the Holy Spirit say to me, "Don't change it." That first post on October 2016 received over 60 comments before the noon hour. That's when I knew I was on to something.

The purpose of God Morning is to inspire, uplift, rejuvenate and assist readers in life's most difficult challenges. I want to encourage them to press onward to victory through developing their personal time with God by applying His word in their everyday lives, thus, allowing the Holy Spirit to do His work in assisting us in becoming the new creation Christ intended.

It is important for us to understand that the power of our words and faith in the power of His word will always lead us to victory. The God Morning devotional is a tool to help us to unlock the small foxes that keep us from obtaining His goal and promise for our lives. As found in Jeremiah 29:11 (NLT), "For I know the plans that I have for you says the Lord. They are plans for good and not for disaster, to give you a future and a hope."

Table of Contents

God Morning,
because He's the One in control of it anyway!

Day 1

Our God Morning Life Lesson: **Unconditional Love.**

"For this is how God loved the world he gave his uniquely existing Son so that everyone who believes in him would not be lost but have eternal life." (John 3:16 ISV)

In Luke 23, it tells the story of a 33-year-old young man by the name of Jesus. The story unfolds as Jesus, who is the Son of God, is faced with the ultimate challenge to complete the task His Father God and Holy Spirit set out for Him to do: to reconcile man back to God, make an escape plan for mankind to bypass damnation and purchase mankind's redemption by way of the cross. It is time to...

STOP ~ for a minute and imagine: would you give up your son, grandson, brother or nephew for the sins of this world? Because of the unconditional love of God our Father and the selfless sacrifice of Jesus. In John 3:16 (ISV), "For this is how God loved the world: He gave his uniquely existing Son so that everyone who believes in him would not be lost but have eternal life." The charges of sin were...

DROPPED ~ against you! I challenge you this morning to read Luke 23:39-43. It is the story of Christ's unconditional love for you and all mankind. As you read about Christ's crucifixion, pay close attention to the dialogue between the two thieves and Jesus. Although a crucial time of His life, Jesus took the time to reassure the condemned soul that his sins were forgiven. Granting him peace, knowing that Jesus would escort him to his resting place – HEAVEN.

LISTEN ~ to the lesson the Holy Spirit teaches us of His "UNCONDITIONAL LOVE."

PRAY ~ that as you turn your eyes upon JESUS you would be able to love, forgive and bring hope to others as our Lord and Savior Jesus Christ demonstrated for us on the cross.

~Pray this Prayer~

Heavenly Father, I thank you for the great sacrifice You and Your Son, Jesus Christ made for me on the cross. Jesus, I ask that Your Holy Spirit open my eyes that I might see the great provision of eternal life You have provided for me. Father, it is because of this great sacrifice that I can boldly approach Your throne of grace to obtain mercy anytime I am in need. Jesus, thank you for paying the penalty of sin for me. I do not deserve such great and unconditional love. Holy Spirit, teach me how to love You, teach me how to love Jesus, teach me how to love the Father and teach me how to love others enough to share the news that eternal life is available to all. In Jesus Name. Amen!

God Morning,

because He's the One in control of it anyway!

Day 2

Our God Morning Life Lesson: **Grief.**

"My flesh and my heart may fail, but God is the strength of my heart and my portion forever." (Psalm 73:26 NIV)

If you live long enough, you will experience grief, pain and sorrow at some point in your life. However, the scripture has an answer for this too. In Psalm 30:5(b), the Psalmist says that, "...in his favor is life: weeping may endure for a night but joy cometh in the morning." It is time to...

STOP ~ and allow your feelings of grief to come to the surface. It's very important to give yourself permission to grieve.

DROP ~ the pretense of pretending to be strong! In your moment of vulnerability and pain, remember you have a much stronger source to lean on. As noted in Psalm 73:26, "My flesh and my heart may fail, BUT God is the strength of my heart and my portion forever."

LISTEN ~ to the language of God's unfailing love and commitment to get you through your time of grief. Finally...

PRAY ~ that you will surrender to the leading of the Holy Spirit to bring life, healing and wholeness back into your life. For he is near to those who are crushed in spirit. Give Him a chance to comfort you. I promise you won't regret it!

~*Pray this Prayer*~

Heavenly Father, my heart is overwhelmed at this moment and I can't seem to find the words to describe how I am feeling. I pray Lord Jesus that You will hear my plea for help to make some sense out of this tragic loss. My heart is ravished with pain and sometimes it is hard to breathe. So, I come to You to help me through Your precious Holy Spirit to breathe fresh upon me. I seek Your face today for guidance and comfort. Your word says that You are near to the broken in spirit. I will make a conscious decision today to look to You to help me through this moment of grief. I will make another decision to trust You throughout this next hour to bring me peace. I choose to allow Your precious Holy Spirit to lead and guide me in Your path of peace, love and security. Thank you, Lord Jesus, that You care and are aware of my pain. Thank you for loving me and not judging me. Thank you for healing me and not dismissing me. Thank you for holding me and not rejecting me when I don't understand this part of Your plan. Thank you, Lord Jesus, for keeping me in perfect peace because I choose to keep my mind steady on You, Your love and mercy. In Jesus Name. Amen!

God Morning,

because He's the One in control of it anyway!

Day 3

Our God Morning Life Lesson: **Restlessness.**

"Come unto me all who are weary and heavy burdened, and I will give you rest. Take my yoke upon you and learn from me, for I am gentle and humble in heart, and you will find rest for your souls." (Matthew 11:28-29)

In Psalm 43:5, the psalmist asks this question, "Why art thou cast down, O my soul? and why art thou disquieted within me? Hope in God: for I shall yet praise him, who is the health of my countenance, and my God." (Psalm 43:5 KJV).

In other words, why are you in distressed? Why are you so restless from within? What is it that has you so agitated that you are losing sleep? What has made you unable to find the rest that has already been provided? Restlessness occurs when we believe that there's an unexpected delay in our hearts for an answer. Isaiah 55:8 helps us with this response to restlessness. The Father says, "For my thoughts are not your thoughts and my ways are not your ways." We become restless when events are happening around us that we don't understand, so we take on the unnecessary burden of becoming restless.

How are we to go about the task of trading our restlessness for his rest? Jesus spoke of exchanging our restlessness for his rest. Now its times to...

STOP ~ and remember that you have control of your thoughts. Controlling your raging thoughts of restlessness will put you on the path of casting your cares onto the One who can bear them. Make the decision to...

DROP ~ any and all behaviors that continue to put you in a state of restlessness.

LISTEN ~ to your inner man to determine the cause of your restlessness. The Holy Spirit will gently remind you that it is His job to bring you comfort and peace. Listen to Him and let Him do his work. Finally, ...

PRAY ~ to the GOD of mercy and grace who has promised in Isaiah 26:3 (TLB), "You will keep him in perfect peace all those who trust in him, whose thoughts turn often to the Lord." Put your faith in the one who has proven to be trustworthy and faithful to His word.

~Pray this Prayer~

Dear Heavenly Father, I come to You in the name of Jesus Christ, my Savior. I ask for Your forgiveness in taking on the cares of my life that I cannot bear alone. Jesus, I ask that Your Holy Spirit lead and guide me into a place of rest. I make the decision to cast my cares upon You today and every day. Putting my faith in You is my real test to rest in You and Your plan for me today. I accept Your rest for my life today, and I will not allow anyone or anything to distract me from resting in You. I pray this in Jesus Name. Amen!

God Morning,
because He's the One in control of it anyway!

Day 4

Our God Morning Life Lesson: **Change Your Mind.**

"Set your mind on things above and not on earthly things."
(Colossians 3:2 NIV)

You have the right to make up your mind as to how your day or life will be! If you're sad, change your mind! You have the mind of Christ and the wisdom of God is within you. Change your mind if you are feeling insecure. The joy of the Lord is your strength! It is time to…

STOP ~ the negativity in your life! Learn how to say "no" to negative people or situations in your life.

DROP ~ the negative attitude about your situation. Complaining only adds fuel to the fire of an already negative attitude. Your attitude determines your altitude! Your negative attitude has the ability to weigh you down, and you're unable to see anything positive in your life.

LISTEN ~ for the joy of laughter around you and allow it to minister to your heart! The word says that laughter does the heart good like medicine.

PRAY ~ that you will continue to move forward throughout this day to change your mind about your negative situations you may encounter.

~*Pray this Prayer*~

Heavenly Father, your word says that I have the mind of Christ and the wisdom of God is formed within me. Jesus, thank you for leading me into a healthy place in my life. Holy Spirit, thank you for showing me how to change my mind and my attitude when things don't go the way I've planned. Thank you, Father, for helping me to grow and mature in this area. Jesus, thank you that I am not alone in this journey of choosing to see the good and concentrate on the positive instead of the bad. Holy Spirit, thank you for training my mind to think on what is good for me, what is positive for me and what is profitable to add to my life daily. In Jesus Name. Amen!

God Morning,

because He's the One in control of it anyway!

Day 5

Our God Morning Life Lesson: **Fear and Chaos.**

"And ye shall hear wars and rumors of wars see that ye be not troubled. For all these things must come to pass, but the end is not yet." (Matthew 24:6 KJV)

The world seems as though it has lost its focus or direction for peace, brotherly love or caring for your neighbor. Fear and chaos are the favorite weapons of our adversary, the father of all lies, Satan himself. In Matthew 24:6 (KJV), Jesus says, "And ye shall hear wars and rumors of wars see that ye be not troubled. For all these things must come to pass, but the end is not yet."

We are to be reminded of what 2 Timothy 1:7 brings us to understand, "For God did not give us a spirit of timidity, but a spirit of power, of love and of self-discipline." God promises in Psalm 138:3 (ESV) that "on the day I called, you answered me; my strength of soul you increased." We must exercise our faith.

In Psalm 16:8 (KJV), David says, "I have set the Lord always before me. Because he is at my right hand, I will not be shaken." Let's take our lesson from Timothy and David and do not accept the fear that the world has to offer. Matthew reminds us that these things must come to pass but we are to be of good cheer and know that what the world may be offering, fear, doubt and pain doesn't mean it's over. The end is not yet. It is time to…

STOP ~ and meditate on the word of God! Make it a way of life to…

DROP ~ to your knees and…

PRAY ~ to the GOD of all hope. Ask the Spirit of God to open your heart and give you an ear to hear…

LISTEN ~ to what the Spirit of God has to say to you today. Remember being strong in the Lord and the power of his might!

~Pray this Prayer~

Heavenly Father, I bow before You in the name of Jesus. I thank you for providing a way of escape from the madness of this world through Your peace. Holy Spirit, I ask in Jesus' name that You will bring clarity to my mind so that I will no longer accept the world's solutions for my life. Peace and tranquility are available to me through You, Holy Spirit. Father, I make a quality decision today to stop allowing fear to rule my heart and mind. Satan will no longer steal my strength, my hope or my dreams. I ready myself to listen closely to Your voice as you lead me down the path of peace, far away from the distractions of this world. In Jesus Name. Amen!

God Morning,

because He's the One in control of it anyway!

Day 6

Our God Morning Life Lesson: **God's Promise.**

"Do not fear, for I am with you; Do not anxiously look about you, for I am your God I will strengthen you, surely I will help you, Surely I will uphold you with My righteous right hand." (Isaiah 41:10 NASB)

What a promise! Isaiah 41:10 is one of the many promises God made in His word. With all the things going on in your life, in the world or in the lives of those around you, it is good to know that you are not alone. God made a promise in Isaiah 41:10 (NASB).

Let's break down what this would mean to you:

- God says, "Do not fear!"
- He reminds us that we are not alone and that He is with us!
- Do not be anxious about the chaotic things that are happening around you!
- Again, He reminds us that He is God!
- He promises without a doubt to strengthen you to give you His strength!
- It's a definite promise that He will surely help you because He reminds us once again that He's there!
- He says that He will uphold you and sustain you! He will lift you up with His righteous right hand and nothing less.

11

So, why worry? Why are we frozen in our current position and not moving forward? God has said over and over that He's got you, your life and everything around you, yet we still doubt and walk in fear? Why? Good question.

Take some time today and meditate on the promise in His word. It's not enough just to read the word. It's imperative that you put action to your words. It is time to...

STOP ~ and take the time to study the word given to you. It's good to confess and admit that you have...

DROPPED ~ the ball and walked more in fear than in faith.

LISTEN ~ to what the promise of God has for you today! You don't have to fear, be anxious or worried about what's surrounding you! Instead, remind yourself as you...

PRAY ~ to the Lord God Almighty who holds you, leads you comforts you and keeps His promise to you. Simply because He can! Trust God, not your circumstances!

~Pray this Prayer~

Father God, in the name of Jesus, I ask that You help me with my negative view of the world and the stress that it has brought to my life. Heavenly Father, today I will not allow myself to be anxious. In doing so, it causes me to lose focus on Your promise to keep me close to You and in Your plan of peace for my life. Holy Spirit, I surrender my thoughts to You and ask that You assist me throughout the day to remain in God's plan of peace for my life today. In Jesus Name. Amen!

God Morning,
because He's the One in control of it anyway!

Day 7

Our God Morning Life Lesson: **Practice What You Preach.**

"Fathers do not provoke your children to anger, but bring them up in the discipline and instruction of the Lord." (Ephesians 6:4 ESV)

How many of you can quote Proverbs 22:6 (NKJV), "Train up a child in the way he should go: and when he is old, he will not depart from it." What about Proverbs 22:15 (KJV), "Foolishness is bound in the heart of a child; but the rod of correction shall drive it far from him."

As parents, we have been quick to discipline our children but have failed to realize that this message is directed at all God's children. Which includes you! Just as we expect our children to trust us when they have made a mistake that needs correcting, God expects us to trust Him in the same way.

Ephesians 6:4 (ESV) says, "Fathers, do not provoke your children to anger, but bring them up in the discipline and instruction of the Lord." God's desire is for us to treat our children in the same way that He treats us with dignity, respect compassion and mercy.

Colossians 3:21 (ESV) echoes, "Fathers, do not provoke your children, lest they become discouraged." It is time to…

STOP ~ a minute to see how God may have been trying to get our attention in regard to our negative behavior. Many times, we may have demonstrated for our children the phrase" do as I say, not as I do." In other words, the unspoken intent of many parents that children follow our instructions, but not "model" our actions! This is exactly what the scripture is telling us regarding foolishness that is bound in the heart of a child! That child is YOU!

DROP ~ the notion of expecting your children to trust you in times when they feel they have failed. However, you do not hold yourself to the same standard when it comes to you facing up to your mistakes before God.

LISTEN ~ by practicing the art of listening to hear what your child has to say about what they are feeling or experiencing when they mess up. Finally, you should…

PRAY ~ that you can become the example of mercy and grace for your children.

~Pray this Prayer~

Father, today I ask that You forgive me when I frustrate and irritate my children due to my lack of patience and gentleness. I thank you Jesus for giving me the opportunity to make corrections in my behavior in dealing with my children. Thank you, Heavenly Father, that You have shown me Your mercy, grace and patience when I didn't deserve it. Today, I will make every attempt to be the example to my children that You desire for me to be. In Jesus Name. Amen!

God Morning,

because He's the One in control of it anyway!

Day 8

Our God Morning Life Lesson: **Fruit of the Spirit.**

"Rejoice in the Lord always; again, I will say, rejoice! Let your gentle spirit be known to all men. The Lord is near."
(Philippians 4:4-5 NASB)

Let your gentle spirit meaning your graciousness, unselfishness, mercy, tolerance and patience be known to all people. The Lord is near. What!! The Lord is serious about His children genuinely displaying the fruit of His Spirit. He desires for His fruit to be a part of our daily behavior and character, especially with those with whom you'd rather just catch an attitude.

He takes it a little further in verse 8 with when he says, "Finally brethren, whatever is true, whatever is honorable, whatever is right, whatever is pure, whatever is lovely, whatever is of good reputation, if there is any excellence and if anything, worthy of praise, dwell on these things."

Center your mind on His character and the fruit of His spirit and implant them in your heart! Practice these things daily so that the God of peace and well-being will be with you. Make the following declarations: I will make the decision to become Spirit-led. It is time to…

STOP ~ trying to figure things and people out. Today, I will…

15

DROP ~ any negative thought, attitude or behavior that can steal away my peace. It's my choice to...

LISTEN ~ to and follow the leading of the Spirit of peace. I will...

PRAY ~ that God will help me to see that I can and will do all things through Christ and His Holy Spirit who strengthens me daily. For we must remember this... that we are His workmanship created in Christ Jesus. Furthermore, we are not our own, but we have been bought with the price of Christ's precious blood who valiantly leads us into victory every time we obey Him and His word.

~Pray this Prayer~

Heavenly Father, I thank you that I can take the pressure off by not trying to figure things out for myself. Holy Spirit, thank you for helping me to understand I can, and I will do all things through Christ who gives me strength daily. Father, I am making a quality decision to make every effort today not to worry about the opinions of others concerning my life. I pray Heavenly Father, that I will make every effort to declutter my mind and my life from negative thoughts, words, people, circumstances and situations that are not adding positive advancement in my life. Today, I will give You praise for always loving and keeping me. Thank you for loving me enough to care about my every need. Holy Spirit, teach me how to adopt to Your character and surrender to Your leadership and guidance. Teach me how to be patient, merciful, and loving toward others. I am forever grateful that I am Your child and that Your presence is always with me. I pray this in Jesus Name. Amen!

God Morning,

Day 9

Our God Morning Life Lesson: **Deception**.

"Let no one deceive you with empty words, for because of these things the wrath of God comes upon sons of disobedience." (Ephesians 5:6 ESV)

Have you heard the expression, "Don't let the green grass fool you?"

Deception is the act of making someone believe something that is not true or the act of hiding the truth, especially to get an advantage. It is lying to trick someone, to steer them away from what the truth in exchange for a lie or something fake. Jesus said in Matthew 24:4 (NASB), "See to it that no one misleads you." Ephesians 5:6 (ESV) takes it a step further, "Let no one deceive you with empty words, for because of these things the wrath of God comes upon sons of disobedience."

Wait a minute, this sounds serious!

This scripture leads us to understand that there is an accountability and responsibility on the one who is deceived. Why, yes! For it says, "*See* to it and *let* no one mislead you." In other words, I'm responsible for my actions if I give up the truth for a lie. Many times, we may know the truth about a person's unscrupulous character and behavior. However, we close our eyes because we don't want to deal with the truth of the matter.

We can set ourselves up to be deceived because we want what we want. Then when things don't turn out the way we've deceived ourselves into believing, we want to cry wolf. There's another side of deception. In John 8:44 (NIV), Jesus tells the Pharisees, "You belong to your father the devil", and you want to carry out your father's desires. He was a murderer from the beginning, not holding to the truth, for there is no truth in him. When he lies, he speaks his native language, for he is a liar and the father of all lies."

We can also believe what John 10:10(a) says, "The thief comes only to steal and kill and destroy." Jesus said, "This is my reason for coming to you, that you might have life and have it to the full." It is time to...

STOP ~ listening to the lies of the enemy, the father of all lies. Allow the Holy Spirit to continue to...

DROP ~ nuggets of truth regarding your confusing and contentious situation. Read John 10:10 out loud and...

LISTEN ~ for the truth of God's word to lead you out of the areas of deception in your life.

PRAY ~ that the eyes of your understanding will be enlightened so you will be able to discern the truth of all matters in your life.

~*Pray this Prayer*~

Heavenly Father, today I have many requests before You. Holy Spirit, in the name of Jesus, I ask the Father's forgiveness for my part in allowing myself to be deceived regarding certain people and situations in my life. Father, I repent before You today. Holy Spirit, help me to see that if I continue down this path of deception, that it is not pleasing to You nor is it healthy for me. I repent for being disobedient to You and deceiving others in my life. Help those I've hurt to find it in their heart to forgive me for my wrongdoing. In Jesus Name. Amen!

God Morning,

because He's the One in control of it anyway!

Day 10
Our God Morning Life Lesson is **Patience.**

"Hot tempers cause arguments, but patience brings peace."
(Proverbs 15:18 GNT)

Have you ever been challenged with people who work in a professional environment yet act like first-year high school students who do not know their way around their new school building?

News flash! Don't get upset with the person at the desk. They have no power. They are at the mercy of the powers that be!

Ephesians 4:2 (GNT) tells us, "Be always humble, gentle, and *patient*. Show your love by being tolerant with one another." Proverbs 15:18 (GNT) says, "Hot tempers cause arguments, but *patience* brings peace."

Now wait a minute! What if they get an attitude first? Am I still required to remain patient and humble? As a human being, am I not entitled to speak my mind or show my frustration, especially in today's climate of short tempers, racism, road rage and the rhetoric coming from the media?

Well, I'm sorry to say the answer to that question is found in 2 Peter 1:5-6 (GNT), "For this very reason do your best to add goodness to your faith; to your goodness add knowledge; to your knowledge add self-control; to your self-control add endurance; to your endurance add godliness..." It hurts to know that even when you're justified, Christ still expects us to be of godly character. The ending of 2 Peter 1:8 (GNT) says, "For in doing so they make you active and effective in your knowledge of our Lord Jesus Christ."

When there are ignorant, annoying behaviors displayed by people around you, remember that Colossians 3:12 (GNT) says, "You are the people of God; he loved you and chose you for his own. So then, you must clothed yourselves with compassion, kindness, humility, gentleness and *patience*." Jesus! Be still my soul! My flesh would much rather let them have a piece of my mind! Even if I wanted to blow off my frustration and pout about how I was inconvenienced, I must halt. This road leads to nowhere. I must stop before I blow off all that steam and unload all that garbage onto someone else. So, with that I will say it is time to...

STOP ~ being upset over what I cannot change. I will...

DROP ~ my negative attitude of anger and frustration and tighten up my shield of faith in order to quench the fiery darts of the enemy who is trying to steal my peace. With that, I will...

LISTEN ~ to the still, small voice of the Holy Spirit to seek His peace and allow it to guard my heart and my mind in Christ Jesus. Finally, I will...

PRAY ~ that this delay is God's plan and that He is in control over every situation and circumstance that I face. I will confess that any delays in my life are orchestrated by God. Therefore, I will sit back and allow Him to take control of my life. I will trust that He has everything under control! Peace and Patience are His virtues.

~Pray this Prayer~

Dear Jesus, I will be the first to admit that I lack patience in several areas of my life. Teach me, Holy Spirit how to add goodness to my faith. Father, sometimes I lose sight of my faith and allow anger and frustration to get the best of me. Today, I make a quality decision to practice loving myself and have patience when things don't seem to be going in the right direction. Today, I make a quality decision to practice loving myself. I choose to practice patience and self-control with those around me. Help me to realize in that moment I want to throw a tantrum, your precious Holy Spirit will gently tug on my heart to surrender to Your will and use self-control. I know I can't always have everything to go my way. However, I know now that if I trust You, You will make a clear path for me to always triumph! In Jesus Name. Amen!

God Morning,

because He's the One in control of it anyway!

Day 11

Our God Morning Life Lesson: Challenges.

"Moses said to the people, "Do not be afraid! Take your stand [be firm and confident and undismayed] and see the salvation of the Lord which He will accomplish for you today; for those Egyptians whom you have seen today, you will never see again." (Exodus 14:13 AMP)

Moses and the children of Israel were faced with multiple challenges that seemed utterly impossible:

1) A mad man, Pharaoh, the Egyptian ruler, was chasing them down to kill them.
2) They escape by the parting of the Red Sea.
3) They mistrusted God's direction for their way out of the wilderness.
4) Confusion and rebellion followed by death.

It was difficult for their minds to perceive how they would overcome such surmounting, impossible odds. However, the God of all hope came to the rescue with clear instructions address their challenges:

1) Do not be afraid.
2) Take your stand.
3) Be firm and confident.
4) Do not be dismayed.
5) Watch for God's handy work.
6) Keep silent and remain calm.

This list seems to make no sense when facing impossible odds. It's difficult to see the victory of the Lord, the one who will fight the battle for you. We are simply to put our challenges to rest when fear arises. It is time to…

STOP ~ being afraid and remember that God has not given you the spirit of fear, but peace and a sound mind. Recognize you have the power within you to…

DROP ~ the feelings of being dismayed, horrified, and unnerved when aroused by a sense by fear and apprehension.

LISTEN ~ with assurance for the voice of the Lord that will lead you back to that place of peace, calmness, rest and confidence in His ability. Know that this is His battle and victory is always the outcome. Finally, …

PRAY ~ that He will keep you in perfect peace as you keep your thoughts continually on His love for you. Remember that His power causes you to be more than a conqueror through Him.

~*Pray this Prayer*~

Father, in the name of Jesus, help me to realize that this battle is not mine to fight, especially not alone. I thank you Holy Spirit that You are leading and guiding me into all truth regarding the giants I face today. Your word reminds me not to be afraid. I will not allow fear to overtake me. You've asked me to stand strong, so today I realize that I am strong in You and in the power of your might. You've asked me to be confident and not to worry. Holy Spirit, I cast my cares upon You because I can trust You with them. Holy Spirit, train my mind and my spirit to listen for Your still, small voice when You are speaking. Help me to remain calm and embrace Your peace today! Victory is just on the horizon, and You will meet me at my point of challenge and struggle and to cause me to win. In Jesus Name. Amen!

God Morning,

because He's the One in control of it anyway!

Day 12
Our God Morning Life Lesson: **A Better You.**

"Therefore, if anyone is in Christ, he is a new creation. The old has passed away; behold, the new has come."
(2 Corinthians 5:17 ESV)

From practically every pulpit, you may hear sermons on various topics such as "Finishing Strong," "Jump Start Your Future," "Let Go So You Can Have an Overflow" or something of the sort. I'd like to pose this question to you: Are you willing to change for the better? Are you willing to slow down for just a moment and give serious thought to how change can take place in your life? Change can only come if you do these things:

1) Recognize there's a need for change.
2) Decide to willingly make change in your life.
3) You decide if you're willing to put in the work to change.
4) Realize that you can only change yourself.
5) Don't look for others to validate your change.

How desperate are you for A Better You?

A Decision to change to become a better you are always accompanied by an action. Recognize that change is never easy. Your future depends on you taking necessary action steps. Scripture tells us in Ecclesiastes 3:1 (ESV) that, "for everything there is a season and a time for every matter under heaven." It is time to...

STOP ~ and ask yourself: Is it my season for change?

DROP ~ the excuses with reasons not to make the necessary changes in your life! Philippians 4:13 (NIV) says, "I can do all things through Christ who strengthens me." In James 1:22 (NIV), the disciple admonishes us by saying, "Do not merely...

LISTEN ~ to the word of the Lord. Do not deceive yourselves. Do what it says." The Word further instructs us that faith without works is dead. Faith comes by hearing and then doing. In Proverbs 10:17 (NIV), the scripture says that, "Whoever heeds discipline shows the way to life, but whoever ignores correction leads others astray." Knowing this wisdom means that it's very important to...

PRAY ~ to the God of wisdom. In doing so, He will give you strength, lead and guide you into all truth and make your crooked places straight. Your journey of change may not always be an easy one. The change journey is a necessary one that you will not take alone. Decide that you will listen to the voice of the Holy Spirit and make up your mind to make a change in your life for the better.

~*Pray this Prayer*~

Heavenly Father, I admit before You today that I desperately need to make some changes in my life. Holy Spirit, I ask You to open my eyes as You lead me and guide me. Prepare me for the changes that are necessary to accomplish what You have designed to take place in my life. Jesus, I ask that You help my mind to settle down to hear only Your instructions today. Jesus, I ask in Your name to equip me with the discipline that is essential to continue to improve my life for the better. Help me, Heavenly Father, to care about the needs of others. However, help me to want to change for me and not just to please those around me. Help me to forgive those who have hurt me in the past. I ask that You forgive me for the hurt I may have caused others. Jesus, I accept my responsibility for change to take place. Holy Spirit, gently remind me that I don't have to do this alone. Help me to be mindful that You are with me leading and guiding me every step of the way. In Jesus Name. Amen!

God Morning,

Day 13

Our God Morning Life Lesson: **Trust.**

"Trust in the LORD with all thine heart; and lean not unto thine own understanding. In all thy ways acknowledge him, and he shall direct thy paths. Be not wise in thine own eyes: fear the LORD, and depart from evil. It shall be health to thy navel, and marrow to thy bones." (Proverbs 3:5-8 KJV)

Trust is having a firm belief in the reliability, truth, ability or strength of someone or something. Healthy relationships are built on the confidence, reliability and trustworthiness in that something or someone for its sustainability. To trust someone is to have confidence or believe in them. Trust is demonstrated when you have faith or certainty in someone or something. Trust is having assurance, conviction or credence; trust is what all good relationships are built on.

Now that's a mouth full! My question to you: In whom or what is trustworthy enough for you to have trust and full confidence in?

This scripture and definition of trust indicates a need for action:

1) Placing your confidence in the One who is trustworthy. (Proverbs 3:5).
2) Do this with all your heart without wavering or second guessing His worthiness. (Proverbs 3:5).

3) Lean on Him and giving assurance to trust Him and knowing you can have confidence that it is the right thing to do. (Proverbs 3:6).
4) Acknowledge Him in every way and with everything with a promise to lead and direct your path. (Proverbs 3:6).
5) Don't be wise in thine own eyes, fearing the Lord and departing from evil. In other words, reverence God and abruptly leave fear and doubt behind! (Proverbs 3:7).
6) Trust in Him is the substance or core that produces your strength and vitality. (Proverbs 3:8).

I have another question: Do you really trust, rely or depend on God with full confidence in Him and His word as described in Proverbs 3:5-8? Pause and think about it. What if you are faced with a life-changing event? Would you be able to reverence God enough to trust Him to leave fear and doubt behind? Today, I ask you to do a bit of soul-searching to find the answer to these questions. It is time to…

STOP ~ rushing through your prayer time and just reading a few scriptures.

DROP ~ the familiarity with this life-changing scripture and apply it appropriately to your life. Truly…

LISTEN ~ and learn from what the Holy Spirit is trying to teach you. Finally…

PRAY ~ that the God of all hope will envelop you and assist you in opening the eyes of your understanding. In doing so, He will be able to direct you in dark and confusing times so that His will may be established in your life. Trusting in Him will produce an even greater confidence in His reliability and trustworthiness to do what He has promised.

~Pray this Prayer~

Heavenly Father, I ask in the name of your dear Son, Jesus, to rescue me from my huge ego of thinking that I can fix things on my own. Holy Spirit, lead me and guide me as I acknowledge Your presence in my life. Holy Spirit, I will rest in the assurance that as I take steps toward trusting in You, the Father and His word. You have promised to make my crooked places straight and lead me in the right path for each situation or circumstance. I choose to trust you. In Jesus Name. Amen!

God Morning,

because He's the One in control of it anyway!

Day 14
Our God Morning Life Lesson: **Spiritual Warfare.**

"For though we live in the world, we do not wage war as the world does. The weapons we fight with are not the weapons of the world. On the contrary, they have divine power to demolish strongholds. We demolish arguments and every pretension that sets itself up against the knowledge of God, and we take captive every thought to make it obedient to Christ." (2 Corinthians 10:3-5 NIV).

It is important for us to understand the need to engage in spiritual warfare. The scriptures teach us that the weapons of our warfare are not of a physical nature. Our adversary is the devil who never fights fair. He uses our own strengths and weakness against us. His job is always to distract, discourage and to lie on every level about any and everything. Our responsibility in this truth is to take charge of our negative thoughts. One of the tricks our adversary uses frequently is to try to pass the lie of defeat onto believers in Christ Jesus. When we recognize the fact that we are already in a place of victory, we can utilize our power over the adversary through the power of our Lord and Savior Jesus Christ.

Have you ever wondered why you were exercising strong faith one minute then, before you know it, your confidence, excitement, and motivation about the things of God suddenly diminish? What just happened to make you feel defeated?

Well, I am here to tell you this is where 2 Corinthians 10:3-5 comes into play.

Therefore, it is so important to guard your heart, your mind and your thoughts. Fear is one of our adversary's finest weapons to put us in a permanent mindset of defeat. In Psalms 27:2 (KJV), David wrote, "When the wicked advance against me to devour me, it is my enemies and my foes who will stumble and fall."

Just remember this acronym for fear: **F**alse **E**vidence **A**ppearing **R**eal. Satan's lies are presented under false pretenses to appear as though they are true. His lies will never be true. It only becomes true if we believe it, confess it or we allow fear to grip our hearts and minds. At this point, we start living as though what we fear is true. It is time to....

STOP ~ listening to the lies going off in your head. Reject the false evidence. Make the decision to...

DROP ~ the negative thoughts, feelings and behaviors. Exchange them for the truth. If God is for you, then who can be against you! Let this mind be in you, which is also in Christ Jesus!

LISTEN ~ to the word of God and let it remind you of your victory through Christ!

PRAY ~ with confidence and boldness, knowing that what you bind on earth has been bound in heaven! Continue to remind the adversary that Jesus is greater than the lies he uses against you to try to distract, discourage or defeat you!

Tell yourself that you're not having it today! For you are not alone Jesus promised to never leave you or forsake you! For you are more than a conqueror through the strength, love and truth of His word working for you and through you!

~Pray this Prayer~

Heavenly Father, in the name of Jesus, I open my heart and my mind to receive your instructions regarding Satan with his bags of tricks and deceit. Let the eyes of my understanding be enlightened to recognize when the enemy is operating in my life. Satan, you were defeated by the victory my Lord and Savior Jesus Christ provided for me on the cross of Calvary. Satan, I refuse to continue to listen to your lies. I will no longer follow after your ways or your works. I have victory over you in the name of Jesus. I am loved by God through His Son, Jesus. I execute the power of that love to extinguish all evil that you brought against me. Holy Spirit, I thank you for providing me with strength and wisdom to defeat my enemy through the power of my Lord and Savior Jesus Christ. I speak these words over my life today in Jesus Name. Amen!

God Morning,
because He's the One in control of it anyway!

Day 15
Our God Morning Life Lesson: **True Love.**

"That Christ may dwell in your hearts through faith. I pray that you being rooted and grounded in love, may have power together with all the saints to comprehend the length and height and depth of His love. To know the love of Christ that surpasses knowledge, that you may be filled with all the fullness of God." (Ephesians 3:17-19 KJV)

"How do I love thee? Let me count the ways! I love thee to the depth and breadth and height my soul can reach." These lines are from "Sonnet #43" by Elizabeth Barrett Browning, a 17th Century Poet. I was first introduced to the poem in my high school English Literature class. I used to recite it to the love of my life, my husband, when we were just teens. Little did I know the true meaning of those words until I met Jesus Christ, my Lord and Savior.

I am inclined to believe that Ms. Browning's inspiration may have been influenced by the scripture found in Ephesians 3:17-19 (KJV), "That Christ may dwell in your hearts through faith. I pray that you being rooted and grounded in love, may have power together with all the saints to comprehend the length and height and depth of His love. To know the love of Christ that surpasses knowledge, that you may be filled with all the fullness of God."

When you read such beautiful words of unconditional love, where does it lead you? Does it lead you to a heart of gratitude and worship? In John 3:16, it emphasizes, "For God so loved the world, that's you and I, so much that He willingly gave His Son for us.

Take a moment to pause and think about the greatest love on earth. God's Love.

I can't help but feel overwhelmed when I think about His love and concern for me. The scripture says in Colossians 3:16(a) NIV, "Let the love of Christ dwell in you richly." That it overflows to the full until you can only see His love for you in the midst of trials, tests or temptations. Scripture further tells us that His perfect love casts out all fear, doubt, worry and unbelief.   You may ask, "What do I have to do to receive this kind of love"?   Well, nothing. Yes, that's right nothing. The love Jesus has for you and me was paid for through His blood sacrifice on Calvary. The only requirement to take possession of His love is to use your faith and believe that He loves you and He wants the best for you.   Believe that His love conquers all, regardless of what you think. Take responsibility to trust and believe that His love is pure and more than enough to carry you through all circumstances, trials or tests. With that, it is time to...

STOP ~ doubting His love for you.

DROP ~ to your knees. Humble your heart with an attitude of humility and worship Jesus.

LISTEN ~ for the truth He has to share with you about His love for you and finally...

PRAY ~ that the Love of God that has been placed in your heart by the Holy Spirit will be released to the very depth of your soul to heal you, bring comfort to you and carry you through to the finish line of VICTORY!

~*Pray this Prayer*~

Holy Spirit, thank you for helping me see how much I am loved by the Father. He loves us so much that we are actually called God's dear children. Help me to be more appreciative of the love sacrifice You made for me. I surrender my heart, my mind, my will and my soul to embrace the love You have given me. Holy Spirit, assist me in demonstrating this wonder gift of love to those that are around me. Father God this day, I bow my heart and my knees to worship You. Jesus, I put my hope and trust in Your wonderful miracle of love. I pray that it will spread throughout my life as I walk in full confidence of Your love. I pray in Jesus Name. Amen!

God Morning,
because He's the One in control of it anyway!

Day 16
Our God Morning Life Lesson: **Peace.**

"Let the peace of Christ rule in your hearts, since as members of one body (family) you were called to peace. And be thankful." (Colossians 3:15 NIV)

Getting together with family during the weekend or for the holidays can sometimes be overwhelming in many ways. Today, I would like to speak to you regarding maintaining your peace.

When in tight quarters, seeing some of your relatives every day or for the first time in years can be exciting, exhausting and challenging all at the same time. I thought we'd explore and expand our need for God's peace during this time when engaging in family activities. Colossians 3:15 (NIV) says "Let the peace of Christ rule in your hearts, since as members of one body (family) you were called to peace. And be thankful." Paul is telling us that we've been called to peace, which may imply that this is not your prime opportunity to bring up the subject of a past debt owed.

For example, are you calling your brother to peace when you remind him that he still owes you money? Are you are calling your aunt to peace when you remind her of the expensive necklace she borrowed and never returned? If you answered 'no,' that's correct! Colossians reminds us that we are called to peace and we should be thankful and submit to it!

In fact, the scriptures further states in Hebrews 12:14 (NIV), "Make every effort to live in peace with everyone and be holy; without holiness, no one will see the Lord!"

Letting the fruit of the Spirit found in Galatians 5:22 (NIV), "Love, joy, *peace,* longsuffering, kindness, goodness and faithfulness have its perfect work in you."

During this time of being up close and personal with your love ones. It is time to...

STOP ~ carrying around your anxiety. In 1 Peter 5:7 (NIV) it says, "Cast all your anxiety on him because he cares for you."

DROP ~ the need to pay back for old wrongs of the past! Instead, 1 Thessalonians 5:15 (NIV) says, "Make sure that nobody pays back wrong for wrong, but always strive to do what is good for each other and for everyone else." Instead of arguing your point to the bitter end...

LISTEN ~ to the voice of the Holy Spirit. Strive and pursue the Spirit of peace to help you calm down and help you to refocus on His love and concern for you. Finally...

PRAY ~ like the Bible encourages us to always do. Pray for your family. Pray that the Spirit of love, peace and harmony will visit your special time of family unity. God desires for us to live in unity and harmony with one another. It has to start with someone. Why not let that someone be you?

~Pray this Prayer~

Father, I pray that the peace of God that surpasses all understanding will guard my heart and my mind through Christ Jesus! Father, in Jesus' name, I make a quality decision to release the stress of family dynamics that attempt to takes my focus off You and Your peace. Father, I ask that I make the right choice to walk away from situations that may try to draw me into negativity. I release and let go of the things that have hurt me in the past. I trust You to keep me focused on Your plan and purpose for my life. Thank you for loving me, forgiving me and keeping me. In Jesus Name. Amen!

God Morning,
because He's the One in control of it anyway!

Day 17
Our God Morning Life Lesson: **Sacrificial Love.**

"Greater love hath no man than this, that a man lay down his life for his friends." (John 15:13 KJV)

Have you ever taken the time to read aloud and meditate on the words from the song "Silent Night?"

> Silent night, holy night! All is calm, all is bright. Round yon Virgin, Mother and Child. Holy infant so tender and mild, sleep in heavenly peace, sleep in heavenly peace (John Freeman Young 1859).

This song has been translated in 140 different languages. It is said that this beautiful tribute to the story of Christ's birth was inspired by Luke 2:4-7(KJV):

> "Joseph also went up from Galilee, out of the city of Nazareth, into Judaea, unto the city of David, which is called Bethlehem; (because he was of the house and lineage of David) To be taxed with Mary his espoused wife, being great with child. And so it was, that, while they were there, the days were accomplished that she should be delivered. And she brought forth her firstborn son, and wrapped him in swaddling clothes, and laid him in a manger; because there was no room for them in the inn."

41

We often talk about the sacrifice of our Lord and Savior Jesus Christ. What about the others that were involved in this miraculous event? Mary was just a young girl, nine months pregnant, and Joseph, her husband, confused in his mind of how this young woman was having a baby and now he would be responsible for another young life.

When you think about that quiet night, that holy night, that night of unconditional love and sacrifice, it is a tribute to the freedom we all share. It is the freedom to love, to hope and to serve others that are in need. Because of those who made the ultimate sacrifice to ensure Jesus Christ's birth, we have the privilege to serve the risen Savior and become a part of the family of God. It is time to…

STOP ~ for minute to think about the sacrifice the three of them made together. Let's…

DROP ~ the façade of all of the hustle and bustle and remember that Jesus is the reason to celebrate life everlasting. Pull up the song, "Silent Night." Close your eyes and…

LISTEN ~ to the lyrics and the melody of this beautiful, prophetic song. Allow the serenity and grace of the song to carry you to a place of gratitude and surrender for the things He has done. Remember to…

PRAY ~ a prayer of praise and thanksgiving for His grace for His mercy, love and sacrifice that without the birth of Jesus Christ, there will be no avenue to salvation.

~*Pray this Prayer*~

Heavenly Father, thank you for touching the hearts of Mary and Joseph with the heart of obedience and sacrifice. Holy Spirit, thank you for demonstrating Your willingness to see us through all difficult situations in our lives. Because of those who made the ultimate sacrifice to ensure Jesus Christ's birth, we have the privilege to serve the risen Savior and become a part of Your family. Jesus, thank you that we have the freedom to love, to hope and to serve others that are in need. I ask You, Holy Spirit, to touch my heart with the spirit of obedience and sacrifice so that others may live. I pray this in Jesus Name. Amen!

Day 18

Our God Morning Life Lesson: **Coping with Lost**

"The Lord is close to the brokenhearted and saves those who are crushed in spirit." (Psalm 34:18 NIV)

Grief is a subject that many of us have experienced at one point or another in our lives. Having to cope with the loss of a loved one or something that was near and dear to you.

There are five stages of grief: denial, anger, depression, bargaining and acceptance. However, within each stage, no one can tell you how long you will experience each stage. Grieving for every individual is different, especially during the holidays. It can be a contributing factor that can trigger one or more of the grieving stages when you least expect it. You might experience intense emotions that you first experienced when you lost your loved one. Emotions can be triggered by...

- Your loved one's birthday
- A familiar song that you shared
- Sights or sounds during the holiday celebration.
- The celebrations of others can trigger grief.
- Attending new events without your loved one

Remind yourself to be prepared for special dates that may be approaching. Plan a distraction for example, visit with friends or loved ones on anniversary days or special occasions. It's important to connect with others that you feel you can draw strength and support from. For instance, your church group, a social club that you may be a part of, scheduled lunch dates with old friends you haven't seen in a while.

It's important to understand that grieving is a natural part of the healing process. If you feel that your grief is more than you can handle don't be afraid to seek out professional help, if needed. There aren't any magic wands or potions that can remove your grief. However, I would like to offer the word of God and the power of His Holy Spirit to bring comfort and clarity to your brokenness.

It's important that you give yourself permission to allow the word of God to enter those dark secret places of pain and hurt. In Psalm 119:151 (NIV) David cries out to the Lord saying, "Yet you are near, Lord, and all your commands are true." Then David declares in Psalm 147:3 (NIV) "He heals the brokenhearted and binds up their wounds." It is time to...

STOP ~ the treadmill in your mind that causes you to pretend that you are done with grieving. No one can tell you when to get over the loss you feel.

DROP ~ the notion that no one cares for you. Understand that Jesus does. Next...

LISTEN ~ to the comforting words of the scriptures and be willing to allow God's word access to your brokenness. Finally...

PRAY ~ to the Father who understands your grief better than anyone else. He gave His son for the very loss you are feeling right now. You have access to Him. Place your grief at His feet. You need to "seek the Lord while he may be found, call on him while he is near" (Isaiah 55:6 NIV). Because your heart is tender and you have humbled yourself before him, He will then pour in just the right amount of healing anointing to get you through the day.

No one says that this journey of pain and sorrow would be easy. However, as you embrace the presence of His Spirit, He will draw you near and tend to the brokenness that seems too big of a task for you to handle on your own. God has promised to love you through your pain and bind up all your wounds.

~Pray this Prayer~

Lord Jesus, today I am calling on the name of the One who understands my grief, my sorrow and my pain. Father, I thank you for Your word in Psalm 34:18 that says, "You are close to the brokenhearted and save those who are crushed in spirit." My spirit is crushed beyond what I am able to bear right now. I ask in the name of Jesus that You will touch the tender and sore areas of my heart. I need You to touch me in a special way by Your Holy Spirit so that my emotions will not to get the best of me. Jesus, you are my healing source. I ask you to touch my broken heart. Mend it with your love and tender mercies. Father, there are times I am faced with the reality that overwhelms me. Thank you for being the healing balm that allows me to make it through another day. In Jesus Name. Amen!

God Morning,
because He's the One in control of it anyway!

Day 19

Our God Morning Life Lesson: **How to Stop Confusion.**

"You will keep him in perfect peace as whose mind is stayed on you. Because he trusts in You." (Isaiah 26:3 NKJV)

It's a great day to be alive and grateful! Do you find yourself having the need to have the answer to every problem you are facing? Are you always trying to figure out the next step? Today, I ask that you take a moment and listen to your thoughts and the conversations going on in your mind. You will see that the source of confusion, frustration and stress is coming from within. It's coming from you!

Isaiah gives the answer to our very own problem. In our focus scripture, there is a promise God has made to us. To keep you in perfect peace means having all the required or desired element, qualities or characteristics; or it means to make something completely free from fault or defects or as close to it as possible.

However, there is a condition: as you keep your mind focused on Him. Why? Because you trust Him. So, if you don't do your part to trust in His ability to be the God of peace in your life, it is fair to say that He would be limited to fulfill His promise causing you to be limited in receiving it. Faith without corresponding action is dead! It is time to…

STOP ~ the confusion and frustration in your life. You must take action and trust that Jesus has the answer that you seek.

DROP ~ the pretense that you can face this situation alone.

LISTEN ~ to the voice of the Holy Spirit and apply His word to every circumstance and situation that may come to challenge you.

PRAY ~ that you will have ears to hear His instructions as you seek Him daily to help you. Today, enjoy life, people, and enjoy His peace.

~Pray this Prayer~

Father, today I am choosing to seek after Your peace. I understand that as I accept Your perfect peace in my life, it gives You space to solve this situation according to Your will and purpose for my life. Jesus, I thank you that the pressure is off, and I now realize I don't have to solve every problem or situation on my own. I can come to You in faith, knowing that through Your perfect peace you have a perfect plan for my life. I rest in knowing this truth from Your word. In Jesus Name. Amen!

God Morning,

because He's the One in control of it anyway!

Day 20

Our God Morning Life Lesson: **Treasures of the Heart.**

"A good man out of the good treasure of his heart brings forth good and an evil man out of the evil treasure of his heart brings forth evil. For out of the abundance of the heart the mouth speaks." (Luke 6:45 NKJV)

What your heart is full of will be the determining factor in how you will relate to others. What's in your heart will lead you in how you respond to crisis situations and how you love or choose not to love. A good person produces good things from the treasury of a good heart. That would only mean that an evil person will only respond to what's stored up in his or heart as well.

It is difficult for us to call someone evil, so in most instances we may overlook a person's behavior or action for fear that we may be casting judgment. However, the scripture says in Psalm 37:30 (NKJV) that, "The mouth of the righteous speaks wisdom, and his tongue talks of justice." In other words, what is right is right and what is wrong is wrong. I'd like to challenge you to do a little soul searching in the matters of your heart today. It is time to…

STOP ~ and ask yourself these questions. Be sure to be honest when answering.

1) What is stored in my heart, good or evil?
2) How do I treat others?
3) Do I make excuses for my wrong doing by blaming others or circumstances to avoid taking responsibility?

After you answer these questions truthfully, you will then be able to...

DROP ~ the blinders from your eyes and see a true depiction of who you really are. You are now equipped to...

LISTEN ~ to the responses of others who may have been trying to get your attention in how good or not so good your relationship is with them. Finally, you will be able to...

PRAY ~ to the Father to lead and guide you in the areas of your heart that may need healing and freedom to be the good and kind person God has designed you to be.

~Pray this Prayer~

Heavenly Father, I ask that you quiet my spirit today. Give me the strength and courage to face the negative things I have stored in my heart unknowingly. Father, help me to face this difficult challenge to reveal my true heart to You. I ask that through Your grace and mercy that You will assist me in letting go of all evil thoughts, actions and behaviors that have become a regular part of my life. Create in me the heart of a good person, create in me the heart of a strong person, and Create in me the heart of a just person. In other words, God create in me the heart of the person You designed and created me to be. In Jesus Name. Amen!

God Morning,

because He's the One in control of it anyway!

Day 21

Our God Morning Life Lesson: **Focus.**

"That we are to set our minds on things above and not on earthly things." (Colossians 3:2)

The scripture says in Colossians 3:2 that we are to set our minds on things above and not on earthly things. We are to not give way to the things and the cares of this world. We can't add anything to our lives by worrying.

I ask this question: What are you focused on today?

What is it that you are expending your energy on? Is it fear, anger, hatred or despair? The scripture tells us in John 14:1(NIV), "Let not your hearts be troubled but believe in God…" Begin to put your hope, faith, desires and expectations on Him and His word. It is time to…

STOP ~ worrying about tomorrow for it will take care of itself according to the will of God and the plan He already has laid out for you.

DROP ~ the stones of hatred and division that only lead you down the path of retaliation, hopelessness and despair.

LISTEN ~ to the Father's voice for He is speaking to you. In Revelation 2:29 (NIV), the scripture tells us, "Whoever has ears, let him hear what the Spirit of the Lord says to the churches." What do you hear in your inner man? Listen closely. If you're not able to hear because you're so restless and disturbed in your heart, then you know it is time to…

PRAY ~ for your spiritual ears to be open and receptive to the Holy Spirit's instructions. Pray and ask forgiveness for yourself and others. Pray for your nation if you feel the need to carry the cares of this world. Pray and repent for giving into fear and anger that is setting you on edge because you've made the decision to put your faith in your frustrations instead of the Prince of Peace. Pray for humility and insight. Pray for the love of God to take first place in your heart. Remember as we give way to His Perfect love, it will dispel all fear.

As you pray for the protection and unity of our nation, look at how the Apostle Paul and King Solomon prayed:

> *Heed the words of Apostle Paul:* "For kings and all those in authority, that we may live peaceful and quiet lives in all godliness and holiness. This is good, and pleases God our Savior…" (1 Timothy 2:2-3 NIV).

> *Heed the Word of the Lord to King Solomon:* "If my people, who are called by my name, humble themselves and pray and seek my face and turn from their wicked ways, then I will hear from heaven and will forgive their sin and heal their land." (2 Chronicles 7:14 NIV).

~Pray this Prayer~

Heavenly Father, help me to refocus my energy and time on the will and plan You have for my life. I ask that You forgive me for worrying about every little detail concerning my life and the lives of those around me. Heavenly Father, I admit that I have worried far too often and too long regarding situations and circumstances that I realize I can't control anyway. Father, I ask that You forgive me for putting more time and energy in people, places and things. Instead I make the decision to focus more on my relationship with You and Your word. Help me, Holy Spirit, to spend more reflective time building my faith in your word and in Your ability and willingness to bring me comfort in my time of need. Thank you, Father, for hearing my prayer and thank you that You are the God that will deliver me from all my fears. In Jesus Name. Amen!

God Morning,

Day 22

Our God Morning Life Lesson: **Resentment**.

"Brethren, I do not count myself to have apprehended; but one thing I do forgetting those things which are behind and reaching forward to those things which are ahead."
(Philippians 3:13-14 NKJV)

I'd like to discuss the meaning of the word resentment. Webster defines it as having ill will, acrimony or bitter indignation at having been treated unfairly. Have you ever felt like you could not move forward in your life? Maybe you've noticed that you're unable to complete personal objectives or goals that you've set. Yet, you find you can turn the world upside down to help others to succeed. You might say to yourself as thoughts of wrongdoing against you flood through your mind, "But I've forgiven them!"

Forgiveness is the process in a long stretch of road to healing. However, resentment is one of the many small foxes that tend to spoil your personal vine of success and keep you with this sense of feeling stuck. You can't move forward. You find that you have developed a repetitive habit of procrastination.

Let's go back to the last part of the definition—having a bitter indignation of one being treated unfairly. What I've discovered in my personal life in some cases, it wasn't because I hadn't forgiven; it was because I had not felt vindicated. I felt cheated out of something that was rightfully mine. The wound was so deep that the cut on the surface was healed, but the core of the injury still needed to be healed. I mentioned earlier about the foxes. Whether big or small, foxes are drawn to spilled blood. It does not matter if blood is newly spilled or dried. Small foxes nibble where it's inconspicuous and the damage goes unnoticed. I would liken small foxes to the hurts and pains of the past. God speaks to us about forgetting our past sins and faults, leaving them behind so we can press forward for the prize!

When the Paul speaks of forgetting those things which are behind and pressing on, forgetting the things that so easily beset you (Philippians 3:13-14); he means that for you to have a future, you must be willing to let go of the past! It is so difficult to do because we want retribution! We want the other person to hurt in the same way that they hurt us.

Believe me, this is not a productive way to live your life. Resentment has a way of stealing your life away, bit by bit. Realize that by remaining in a state of resentment, you are refusing to forgive and let go. You are remaining a prisoner of the past. It is time to…

STOP ~ living in your past hurt. Discover the freedom it brings to…

DROP ~ the unproductive behaviors of procrastination and idleness. Take the time to…

LISTEN ~ to your inner man and give yourself permission to move on with your life. Finally…

PRAY ~ that in time as you take back your right to be free you will also be able to release yourself from a place of resentment.

~*Pray this Prayer*~

Heavenly Father, in the name of Your Son, Jesus, I come to You today and confess my sin of anger and resentment. Father, You know the pain that I am experiencing and the hurt and fear that is controlling my life at this moment. Father, in the name of Jesus, help me to understand that just because I choose to forgive doesn't mean I have to allow the hurt to continue in my life. Jesus, I admit this is difficult for me, but I know that all things are possible through You. Today, I will take control of my life by forgiving and reaching forward to those things which are ahead—a future without fear, anger and resentment. I pray this in Jesus Name. Amen!

God Morning,

because He's the One in control of it anyway!

Day 23

Our God Morning Life Lesson is **Love and Attitude.**

"If I had the gift of being able to speak in other languages without learning them and could speak in every language there is in all of heaven and earth, but didn't love others, I would only be making noise. If I had the gift of prophecy and knew all about what is going to happen in the future, knew everything about everything, but didn't love others, what good would it do? Even if I had the gift of faith so that I could speak to a mountain and make it move, I would still be worth nothing at all without love. If I gave everything I have to poor people, and if I were burned alive for preaching the Gospel but didn't love others, it would be of no value whatever. Love is very patient and kind, never jealous or envious, never boastful or proud, never haughty or selfish or rude. Love does not demand its own way. It is not irritable or touchy. It does not hold grudges and will hardly even notice when others do it wrong. It is never glad about injustice, but rejoices whenever truth wins out. If you love someone, you will be loyal to him no matter what the cost. You will always believe in him, always expect the best of him, and always stand your ground in defending him." (1 Corinthians 13: 1-7 TLB)

Can you say OUCH? If we are honest with ourselves, we can clearly see how our fleshy or carnal nature has dominated most of the areas in our lives. This scripture teaches us to grow and to be free to love in a healthy way. How do you love others God's way? By checking your attitude. It is time to…

STOP ~ with the excuses. Stop minimizing the effect your negative attitude is contributing to your situation. Remember the instructions in our focal scripture…

DROP ~ the negative attitude in how you treat others. Recognize that Christ expects us to check our attitude at the altar. Lay aside every weight that would cause you to act apart from the character of Christ.

LISTEN ~ and begin to apply to your daily life and challenges as you read out loud what Paul is saying to you about love and how you treat others. Finally…

PRAY ~ that God will help you to forgive those who have hurt you in the past. Take Paul's advice: "…but one thing I do forgetting those things which are behind and reaching forward to those things which are ahead." (Philippians 3:13 NKJV) The word is written to assist you to build character and to begin to love. In turn, you will be able to love with a healthy love. So that your loved ones won't have to suffer for what someone else did to you.

~Pray this Prayer~

Heavenly Father, I take this time to thank you for loving me with such unconditional love. Thank you for being understanding and patient with me, even when I have not been so with others. Jesus, it is hard to trust others and I admit I have not always put my trust in You when times are difficult for me. Holy Spirit, teach me how to love and have patience. Teach me how to hear Your voice and not rely on just my intellect. I surrender my heart, mind, soul and will to You today. I believe that I can count on You to help lead me through these uncharted waters. Holy Spirit, create in me a willing heart to release the hurts and pains of the past and develop the Christ like character You intended for me. In Jesus Name. Amen!

God Morning,

because He's the One in control of it anyway!

Day 24

Our God Morning Life Lesson: **Control Your Atmosphere.**

"Do not fret because of those who are evil or be envious of those who do wrong; for like the grass they will soon wither, like green plants they will soon die away. Trust in the LORD and do good; dwell in the land and enjoy safe pasture." (Psalms 37:1-2 NIV)

We listen to the newsreels and watch as the rhetoric unfolds. With each revelation more and more fear appears to be unleashed in the atmosphere. Powerlessness seems to set in. In the event this is your current state of mind, David gives some specific instructions that we can follow to elevate and dispel our fears and grave concerns regarding today's perils. In Psalm 37:1-8, David expresses that we should not fret, not to be envious, trust in the Lord, do good, commit your way as well as rest in the Lord and wait and be patient. He continues to tell us to cease from anger, forsake wrath, dwell in the land, feed on His righteousness and delight in the Lord. He expresses it's important to rest in the Lord and wait patiently for Him.

The beautiful part about all of this is after we've done our part, there are some specific promises you can expect to receive from God. When men are workers of iniquity, it's not our job to correct them. God has a system in place called the law of reciprocity. If you do evil, you will reap evil. It's inevitable that you will reap what you sow. They will soon be cut down like grass and wither.

He promises to deliver us from wicked men, and those who plot to do evil against us and who transgress against the righteous shall be punished. However, notice the emphasis is not on the one who's done or is doing evil, the importance of this passage is to remind the believer who is in charge – God. You should focus your attention on Him.

For in doing so, God promises the believer that He will give you the desires of your heart. He shall bring to past the request you've made in faith because you trust in Him and not trust in the system of man. God will not leave us in the hand of the wicked. The salvation of the righteous is from the Lord. He is our strength in the time of trouble. The Lord shall save all who trust in Him. It is time to…

STOP ~ allowing fear to control your atmosphere. Fear is only False Evidence Appearing Real.

DROP ~ to your knees daily and learn how to…

LISTEN ~ to the words of the author and developer of your faith. In doing so, the Holy Spirit will train your ears, your heart and your mind how to utilize the word of God and follow His instructions. Finally…

PRAY ~ to the Father that He will teach you how to pray for those who have rule over us. Pray that you will be able to take control of your feelings of fear. Pray that your heart will not be filled with anguish or despair. Pray that you will find hope and safety in the promises of God.

~Pray this Prayer~

Heavenly Father, you said for us to "pray for our leaders and those who are in authority over us. Heavenly Father, I pray for all mankind today. I ask that You will be with my neighbor, my coworkers, my friends and associates. I ask that You provide the necessary things that they need today. Father, I pray for the President, the Governor, Mayor, school administrators, Sunday School teachers, Pastors and the like. Father, I pray that You will be with the men and women that make decisions and impact our daily lives. I pray that they will rule with peace, wisdom, love and compassion for the people they serve. Father, I thank you for giving my family and me peace concerning our daily lives. Thank you for meeting our needs today. I am thankful for all the provisions You have provided. I thank you that we will work to live our lives that would be pleasing to You as we worship and give You praise today. Thank you that this is the day that You have made and I will rejoice and be glad in it. I pray this in Jesus Name. Amen!

God Morning,
because He's the One in control of it anyway!

Day 25

Our God Morning Life Lesson: **God's Mercy and Grace.**

*"Let us the approach God's throne of grace with confidence,
so that we may receive mercy and find grace to help us in
our time of need." (Hebrews 4:16 NIV)*

In a conversation regarding God's mercy and His grace, the
following passage came to mind. In Exodus 33:18-19 (NIV),
Moses said, "Now show me your glory." And the Lord said,
"I will cause all my goodness to pass in front of you, and I
will proclaim my name, the Lord, in your presence. I will have
mercy on whom I will have mercy, and I will have
compassion on whom I will have compassion." Before our
time here on earth, mercy was made available to us. God's
desire is for us to know that through His divine love, He has
made mercy and compassion available. We are human and we
make mistakes. But God is a loving and forgiving God. It is
His desire for us to know that He provided a way of escape
for the sins we commit against Him, ourselves and those
around us. His mercy is free to us at a cost that His Son, Jesus
paid with His life on the cross. It is His will that we learn from
Him and extend grace as we show compassion and mercy on
those whom we may think may not deserve it! Just remember
this, we didn't deserve it, either. It is time to…

STOP ~ and read this passage. Allow this word to…

DROP ~ the wisdom and compassion deep into your heart.

LISTEN ~ as the Spirit leads you to apply grace and mercy in the lives of those around you.

PRAY ~ for that His mercy and compassion will continue to lead and guide you throughout this day.

~Pray this Prayer~

Heavenly Father, thank you that your grace is sufficient since I fall short of it daily. Thank you for demonstrating your power through grace and mercy, especially in my time of weakness. I ask that you will forgive me in times when I have failed to extend the same gift of grace to others. Holy Spirit, I ask that you will continue to humble me before the throne of God's grace to obtain help when I need it most. Today, I will make a decision to extend grace, hope, love and compassion to others around me. I pray this in Jesus Name. Amen!

God Morning,

because He's the One in control of it anyway!

Day 26

Our God Morning Life Lesson: **Another Season on the Horizon**.

"There is a time for everything, and a season for every activity under the heavens." (Ecclesiastes 3:1 NIV)

In April 2018, while the rest of the country was experiencing springtime weather, the entire state of Minnesota received over 18 inches of snow. On the snowiest day of that week, my sister who lives in the South, where it's warm ten months out of the year, called and wished me a Merry Christmas. I chuckled as the poor squirrels outside my window darted to and fro; just as confused and unhappy as we were. Although we were experiencing winter elements, it was springtime.

Sometimes in our lives, it may look like it's snowing, but another season is on the horizon. We may not like the snow, and we may not enjoy the cold! Oftentimes, we are experiencing what may appear to be hardship when, in fact, the Father is working His master plan when we least expect it.

It is important for us to always remember our most challenging days. It's still a day that the Lord has made and we are to rejoice and be glad in it! Look at it this way. God has given you the opportunity to live and enjoy life as he has designed. Remember the old saying "Don't judge a book by its cover." Just because the cover of the book is not appealing to the eye doesn't mean that the words enclosed are not life changing. It is time to...

STOP ~ for just a minute and take inventory of the things you have prejudged that had a favorable outcome when you least expected. Take this time to stop prejudging your current experiences and...

DROP ~ the unrelenting schedule that may be keeping you and causing you to miss opportunities God has planned for you. It's also good to take this opportunity for some much-needed "me" time.

LISTEN ~ to the silent, peaceful space you've created in your home. Finally...

PRAY ~ that you, your family and friends will remain safe and enjoy this day despite any unfavorable weather outside or inside. You have a job to do, which is to make it shine in your heart, in your home and in your family. It's your special day that the Heavenly Father saw fit to give you, so enjoy it.

~*Pray this Prayer*~

Heavenly Father, this is a day that You have made and designed especially for me. Holy Spirit, help me to remember this when I face challenges throughout the day that may not seem to be going in my favor. To everything there is a season, and a time to every purpose under the heaven. I will trust You even when I don't understand the ins and outs of this day. Jesus, in this season I know the plans you have for me has already been worked out. I make the decision to honor You today and to remain in an attitude of worship, praise and thanksgiving despite the outcome. In Jesus Name. Amen!

God Morning,
because He's the One in control of it anyway!

Day 27
Our God Morning Life Lesson: **Reverence.**

"O Lord, you are my God; I will exalt you, I will give thanks to your name; For you have worked wonders, Plans formed long ago, with perfect faithfulness." (Isaiah 25:1 NASB)

Reverence means to revere, respect, to hold in awe, to adore, to honor, to be afraid of, to become aware of, esteem, treat with respect value or pay homage to.

My question is what or to whom do you reverence? Is it God or something or someone else? It is important to understand that what you fear and reverence the most will get the best part of you. Thanksgiving says to be thankful for what you've been given and to share the blessings of what you've been given. In Psalm 111: 10 (ESV) it says, "The fear of the Lord is the beginning of wisdom; all those who practice it have a good understanding. His praise endures forever!" Finally, intercession. You must spend time praying and petitioning God on behalf of others and stop putting what you need and want always on the forefront of your mind. It is time to...

STOP ~ and take inventory of what or to whom you are giving your best, is it or are they worthy of it?

DROP ~ the things that get you off focus. By doing so, it will lead you back to the one that matters most, Jesus.

LISTEN ~ to the voice of reasoning, it will lead to understanding and clarity in chaotic situations. In turn, it will save you a lot of heartache and wasted energy. Finally...

PRAY ~ and intercede to be in the place that will lead and give you guidance, peace, direction and focus to truly learn how to reverence God. By doing so, you will give Him what He so rightly deserves, which is all of you.

~Pray this Prayer~

Heavenly Father, Creator of all heaven and earth, I praise Your name and lift it high above all things. I reverence Your awesome presence in my life. We are instructed to only fear the Lord and to serve You with truth in our hearts. I will be mindful of all the great things You have done for me. I thank you for all that You have given me, and all the wonderful things I look forward to as I reverence Your Holy and Divine Name. I pray this in Jesus Name. Amen!

God Morning,

because He's the One in control of it anyway!

Day 28

Our God Morning Life Lesson: **Silence.**

"Be still and know that I am God. I will be exalted among the nations. I will be exalted in the earth." (Psalm 46:10 NIV)

Webster defines silence as the complete absence of sound, quietness, tranquility or peacefulness. How many of us can truly say that we have taken the time out from the rhetoric and noise around us to take a moment to completely absorb ourselves in the sound of nothingness? Silence for many can be deafening, but for others, it is soothing, insightful and peaceful. Others are afraid to be alone with silence.

However, God instructs through His word in Psalm 46:10 (NIV), "Be still and know that I am God. I will be exalted among the nations. I will be exalted in the earth." Have you ever stopped and asked yourself why we would need to be still to know that God is God?

God wants us to have hope and put our trust in His power and ability to be God in circumstances that are out of our control. This truth, can only come through SILENCE before Him. It is time to...

STOP ~ and take a moment to bring quietness and serenity to your life.

DROP ~ all the loud rhetoric that continues to draw you away from the truth of how great God is.

LISTEN ~ don't be afraid to listen to the silence, for in it are instructions, healing, hope and restoration for your life. And finally...

PRAY ~ for your Sovereign Lord to lead and guide you into all truth; however, be sure you're ready to listen to His instructions and be willing to be obedient to His word.

~Pray this Prayer~

Heavenly Father, in the name of Your Son, Jesus, I ask that You quiet my mind today that I might hear Your voice. Holy Spirit, lead me through Your still and quiet waters so that my soul can be renewed and regenerated through Your power of peace and tranquility. Holy Spirit, prepare me for the truth You will reveal as I sit quietly before You. Holy Spirit, thank you that You are walking with me as I discover newfound truth in my life. Lord, you will fight for me while I keep still. Thank you for making crooked places straight in my life and helping me to realize I don't have to fight my battles in my mind for You have given me the victory. In Jesus Name. Amen!

God Morning,

because He's the One in control of it anyway!

Day 29

Our God Morning Life Lesson: **Composure.**

"And the peace of God which transcends all understanding and will guard your hearts and your minds in Christ Jesus."
(Philippians 4:7 NIV)

Composure is the state or feeling of being calm and being in control of oneself. It is to be at peace or free from disturbance. We can safely say that when we ask for God's peace, we are asking Him to:

1) keep us calm.
2) help us keep our composure in difficult situations.
3) be free from the disturbance of our disruptive situations.
4) be restful.
5) help us deal with our negative situations with equanimity.
6) keep us steady and positive in any situation.

So, the next time you need to keep your composure when facing adversity remember what you are praying for. It is time to...

STOP ~ and get your mind focused on His promise to give you peace.

DROP ~ the thing(s), situations or people that are disturbing your peace.

LISTEN ~ to the mind of Christ that He has given you. Rest in thoughts of peace, victory and success. He made you a conqueror.

PRAY ~ that the Holy Spirit will keep you in perfect peace as you purposefully keep your mind steady on Jesus and His word.

~Pray this Prayer~

Heavenly Father, today I will follow Your plan according to Colossians 3:15. Father, teach me how to let the peace of Christ rule in my heart since as members of one body I was called to peace and to be thankful. In the name of Jesus, I will make every effort to keep my composure, to live in peace with everyone and to be holy with the help and guidance of Your Holy Spirit. Thank you that as I pursue Your peace to maintain my composure, you have promised to help me deal with any negative or unfavorable situation I may come up against. Father, thank you for loving me so much that You consider my wellbeing. In Jesus Name. Amen!

God Morning,

because He's the One in control of it anyway!

Day 30

Our God Morning Life Lesson: **Powerlessness.**

"The Lord is my light and my salvation whom shall I fear? The Lord is the stronghold of my life of whom shall I be afraid? When the wicked advance against me to devour me, it is my enemies and my foes who will stumble and fall. Though an army besiege me, my heart will not fear; though war break out against me, even then I will be confident."
(Psalm 27: 1-3 NIV)

The world is in disarray. Families are divided and fighting among one another. Money is funny, and health issues are on the rise. Just thinking about this can cause anxiety and for some, a sense of powerlessness and hopelessness for others. You can take control of your situation. How? In 2 Chronicles 7:14 (KJV) it says, "If my people, which are called by my name, shall humble themselves, and pray, and seek my face, and turn from their wicked ways. Then will I hear from heaven, and will forgive their sin, and will heal their land." Ephesians reminds us that our opponent is not of this world. Our spiritual enemies are not of human origin, but they have been commissioned as principalities, powers, rulers of darkness and spiritual wickedness in high places. However, as believers in the power of Jesus Christ, we can pull down these strongholds and render them powerless and ineffective. It is time to…

STOP ~ being afraid. Luke 1:37 (NASB) reminds us, "For nothing will be impossible with God."

DROP ~ to your knees and apply Ephesians 3:20 (NASB), "Now to Him who is able to do far more abundantly beyond all that we ask or think, according to the power that works within us." Then…

PRAY ~ the prayer of faith that can move mountains and change situations.

LISTEN ~ to your heart and what the Spirit of the Lord is speaking to you. We're only as powerless as we allow our circumstances and situations to dictate to us. Take up your shield of faith and quench every fiery dart of the wicked one. The same power that raise our Lord and Savior is available to us. The question is will we use them, or will we continue to stand by and let the enemy paint pictures of lies in our minds and all of those around us?

~Pray this Prayer~

Father, today I make the decision to put Psalm 37:1-5 into action. I will not fret because of those who do evil. Instead I will be strong in you and the power of Your might. I will no longer allow myself to be envious against those whom seem to have the upper hand. Father, Your word says that they shall soon be cut down like the grass, and wither as the green herb. Father, I Trust that You would do good toward me in spite of those around me. I delight in the Lord: and You shall give me the desires of my heart. I Commit my way unto You Lord; I will continue to trust You and You shall bring it to pass. In Jesus Name. Amen!

God Morning,
because He's the One in control of it anyway!

Day 31
Our God Morning Life Lesson: **Where's Your Faith?**

"Now faith is the substance of things hoped for
and the evidence of things not yet seen." (Hebrews 11:1)

Have you ever experienced a time in your life where you wondered if God still is in control of your situation? Have you ever felt like giving up or giving into unbelief and the negative side? Well, welcome to being human and the first lesson of Christianity 101. If you've walked this Christian journey for any length of time, you will experience setbacks in times when you question your faith as well as God's ability to fulfill the promise He made.

Let's remember if God be for you who can be against you? What comes out of your mouth can and will become a reality. Job 22:28(NIV) says, "You can decree a thing and it shall be established." Deuteronomy 31:6 (NIV) says, "Be strong and courageous. Do not be afraid or terrified because of them, for the LORD your God goes with you; He will never leave you nor forsake you."

It is past time for God's people to follow the instructions of Isaiah 41:10 (NIV), "So do not fear, for I am with you; do not be dismayed, for I am your God. I will strengthen you and help you; I will uphold you with my righteous right hand." It is time to…

STOP ~ doubting God's word and put your faith in action.

DROP ~ the weapons of self-sabotage and believe in the God who keeps His promise.

LISTEN ~ And watch out for the enemy who is the father of all lies.

PRAY ~ that the Holy Spirit will give you discernment regarding everything concerning your life and your relationship with Him.

~*Pray this Prayer*~

Heavenly Father, I speak forth Your truth in my life. I believe that all things are possible with You and through You. I will stop allowing the lies of the enemy to dictate my day or the events I will encounter in my life. I can and I will do all things through Christ who gives me strength daily. Thank you, God, for keeping Your promise to never leave me or forsake me. I am not a quitter because You won't quit on me. I am an overcomer because You are my daily help and strength and I have the victory in Jesus Name. Amen!

God Morning,
because He's the One in control of it anyway!

A Daily Reminder
Our God Morning Life Lesson: **Love the Lord your God.**

"Love the Lord your God with all your heart and with all your soul and with all your mind and with all your strength."
(Mark 12:30 NIV)

Love the Lord your God with all of your might, your strength, and breath you breathe. To love God is to be intoxicated with worshipping Him, reverencing Him, serving Him, obeying Him and thanking Him. Recognize that He is the One and Only True and Living God! Trust in Him and Him alone. Understand that how He operates in your life is not predicated on what you think you need. However, it is according to the truth that Jesus died for you on purpose. He loved you before you were aware that you even existed.

On many occasions in our lives, we may not understand where the Father is leading us. The key word here is LEAD! I've discovered over the years that His word really is true and He ALWAYS has my best interest in mind. It is time to...

STOP ~ trying to control my life and let His precious Holy Spirit lead and guide you into all truth. Understanding that it is important that you...

DROP ~ the plans that you have for my life and seek Him daily with all diligence, so that He can reveal to you the plans that He has for you. Learn to...

LISTEN ~ to the voice of the Holy Spirit and develop a lifestyle of obedience to His voice. Finally, learn to...

PRAY ~ using His word to reveal the plans that are laid out for you according to His will, His purpose, His love, His mercy, His grace and His favor that He specifically designed for you. Trust in the Lord your God with all your heart, worship Him in Spirit and in truth. Lean not unto your own understanding. It will help make the journey a little easier, not perfect. Know that you can rest in His arms because He said He will never leave you nor will He ever forsake you. Enjoy your morning and remember to thank Him for this day.

Read the entire chapter of Proverbs 3; it will bless you.

~Pray this Prayer~

Heavenly Father, I will trust You with all my heart, and I will stop leaning and depending on my own understanding. In everything, I will do my best to submit to You. Holy Spirit, thank you that God's love is rooted deep in my heart, and I choose to surrender to His love daily. Teach me how to love You, reverence You and walk daily in obedience to Your love. Jesus, thank you for loving me so very much that You gave Your life so that I can live. Heavenly Father, I'm thankful for my loved ones who love me, especially I am thankful that I have faith and friends and a life to live. I am thankful for God's love, mercy and grace He shows me every day. I'm just thankful. In Jesus Name. Amen!

Prayer of Salvation by Dr. Bryan K. Cole

Understanding what salvation is:

Salvation is a spiritual exchange or encounter with God the Father and creator of heaven and earth.

Salvation is the act of God's mercy, the ultimate redemptive act of God's love through the birth, death, burial and resurrection of Jesus Christ.

When we ask God for the gift of salvation, we're exercising our free will to acknowledge that we believe and trust and accept Him. That demonstration of faith pleases God, because we have freely chosen to accept Him.

When you are ready to become a Christian, you are ready to have your first real conversation with God.

~The Prayer of Salvation~

God, for too long I have kept you out of my life. Heavenly Father, today I come before you recognizing that I have been living life on my own and I have not included you. I know that I am a sinner and that I cannot save myself. No longer will I keep the door closed when I hear you knocking. By faith, an act of my free will, I am ready to trust you as my Lord and Savior. Thank you, Lord Jesus, I believe you are the Son of God who died on the cross for my sins and rose from the dead. Thank you for taking away my sins and giving me the gift of eternal life, Lord Jesus, I choose you as my Lord and my Savior. Amen.

Glossary

Trinity: The Christian Godhead as one God in three persons: Father, Son, and Holy Spirit.

God: The first person of the Holy Trinity the creator of heaven, earth and all mankind. He is referred to as Father or God in this devotional.

Jesus: The second person of the Trinity. Jesus the only begotten Son of God, The Savior of the world.

Holy Spirit: The third person of the Trinity. A unique person not simply a power or an influence, God's personal presence He is described as our comforter and teacher.

Prayer: God has established prayer as the means by which we receive his supernatural help. God's form of communication.

Faith: Complete trust or confidence in someone or something. A strong belief in God or in the doctoring of a religion.

Grace: The free and unmerited favor of God.

Mercy: Compassion or forgiveness shown toward someone whom it is within one's power to punish or harm.

Anointing: The ritual of pouring over a person's head or entire body. A divine influence or presence.

Salvation: The act of God's mercy, the ultimate redemptive act of God's love through the birth, death, burial and resurrection of Jesus Christ.

Redemption: The act of saving someone from sin or evil. The state of being saved from sin or evil. Something that saves someone or something from danger or a difficult situation.

Resurrection: Christ Jesus the Son of God raised from the dead.

Scripture References

Each Scripture Denotes the Bible translation referenced.

John 3:16 ISV – "For this is how God loved the world he gave his uniquely existing Son so that everyone who believes in him would not be lost but have eternal life."

Psalm 73:26 KJV – "My flesh and my heart may fail, but God is the strength of my heart and my portion forever."

Matthew 11:28-29 NIV – "Come unto me all who are weary and heavy burdened, and I will give you rest. Take my yoke upon you and learn from me, for I am gentle and humble in heart, and you will find rest for your souls."

Psalm 30:5(b) KJV – "In his favor is life: weeping may endure for a night but joy cometh in the morning."

Psalm 73:26 NIV – "My flesh and my heart may fail, BUT God is the strength of my heart and my portion forever."

Psalm 43:5(a) NKJV – "Why are you cast down oh my soul? Why are you disquieted within me?"

Isaiah 55:8 GW – "For my thoughts are not your thoughts and my ways are not your ways."

Isaiah 26:3 TLB – "You will keep him in perfect peace all those who trust in him, whose thoughts turn often to the Lord."

Matthew 24:6 KJV – "And ye shall hear wars and rumors of wars, see that ye be not troubled. For all these things must come to pass, but the end is not yet."

Timothy 1:7 NLT – "For God did not give us a spirit of timidity, but a spirit of power, of love and of self-discipline."

Psalm 138:3 ESV – "On the day I called, you answered me my strength of soul you increased."

Psalm 16:8 KJV – "I have set the Lord always before me. Because he is at my right hand, I will not be shaken."

Isaiah 41:10 NASB – "Do not fear, for I am with you; Do not anxiously look about you, for I am your God I will strengthen you, surely I will help you, Surely I will uphold you with My righteous right hand."

Proverbs 22:6 NKJV – "Train up a child in the way he should go: and when he is old, he will not depart from it."

Proverbs 22:15 KJV – "Foolishness is bound in the heart of a child; but the rod of correction shall drive it far from him."

Ephesians 6:4 ESV – "Fathers, do not provoke your children to anger, but bring them up in the discipline and instruction of the Lord."

Colossians 3:21 ESV – "Fathers, do not provoke your children, lest they become discouraged."

Philippians 4:4 KJV – "Rejoice in the Lord always again I say rejoice!"

Matthew 24:4 NASB – "See to it that no one misleads you."

Ephesians 5:6 ESV – "Let no one deceive you with empty words, for because of these things the wrath of God comes upon sons of disobedience."

John 8:44 NIV – "You belong to your father the devil, and you want to carry out your father's desires. He was a murderer from the beginning, not holding to the truth, for there is no truth in him. When he lies, he speaks his native language, for he is a liar and the father of all lies."

John 10:10(a) NIV – "The thief comes only to steal and kill and destroy; I have come that they may have life, and have it to the full."

Ephesians 4:2 GNT – "Be always humble, gentle, and PATIENT. Show your love by being tolerant with one another."

Proverbs 15:18 GNT – "Hot tempers cause arguments, but Patience brings peace."

2 Peter 1:5 GNT – "For this reason do your best to add goodness to your faith; to goodness add knowledge and to your knowledge self-control."

2 Peter 1:8 GNT – "For in doing so they make you active and effective in your knowledge of our Lord Jesus Christ."

Colossians 3:12 GNT – "You are the people of God; he loved you and chose you for his own. So then, you must clothe yourselves with compassion, kindness, humility, gentleness and patience."

Ecclesiastes 3:1 ESTV – "For there is a season and a time for every matter under heaven."

Philippians 4:13 ESV – "I can do all things through Christ who strengthens me."

James 1:22 NIV – "Do not merely listen to the word, and so deceive yourselves. Do what it says."

Proverbs 10:17 NIV – "Whoever heeds discipline shows the way to life, but whoever ignores correction leads others astray."

1 Corinthians 13: 1-5, 7 TLB – "If I had the gift of being able to speak in other languages without learning them and could speak in every language there is in all of heaven and earth, but didn't love others, I would only be making noise. [2]If I had the gift of prophecy and knew all about what is going to happen in the future, knew everything about everything, but didn't love others, what good would it do? Even if I had the gift of faith so that I could speak to a mountain and make it move, I would still be worth nothing at all without love. [3]If I gave everything I have to poor people, and if I were burned alive for preaching the Gospel but didn't love others, it would be of no value whatever. [4]Love is very patient and kind, never jealous or envious, never boastful or proud. [5]Love is never naughty or selfish or rude. Love does not demand its own way. It is not irritable or touchy. It does not hold grudges and it would hardly notice when others do it wrong. [7]If you love someone you will be loyal to him no matter what the cost. You will always believe in him, always expect the best of him, and always stand your ground in defending him."

Philippians 3:13-14 NKJV – "Brethren, I do not count myself to have apprehended; but one thing I do forgetting those things which are behind and reaching forward to those things which are ahead."

John 1:1a NIV – "Let not your hearts be troubled, believe in God."

Luke 6:45 NKJV – "A good man out of the good treasure of his heart brings forth good; and an evil man out of the evil treasure of his heart brings forth evil. For out of the abundance of the heart fis mouth speaks."

Joshua 24:15 NIV – "But if serving the lord seems undesirable to you, then choose for yourselves this day whom you will serve beyond the Euphrates, or the gods of the Amorites, in whose land you are living. But as for me and my household, we will serve the Lord."

Roman 8:31 NKJV – "What then can we say to these things? If God be for us who can be against us?"

John 16:33 NKJV – "These things i have spoken to you, that in me you may have peace. In the world you will have tribulation; be of good cheer i have overcome the world."

Psalm 91:11 NKJV – "For he shall give his angels charge over you, to keep you in all your ways."

Isaiah 26:3 NKJV – "You will keep him in perfect peace as whose mind is stayed on you. Because he trusts in you."

Psalm 34:18 NIV – "The Lord is close to the brokenhearted and saves those who are crushed in spirit."

Psalm 119:151 KJV – "But you are near Oh Lord and all your commandments are true."

Psalm 147:3 NIV – "He heals the brokenhearted and binds up their wounds."

Isaiah 55:6 NIV – "Seek the Lord while he may be found, call on him while he is near."

Luke 2:4-7 KJV – "And Joseph also went from Galilee out of the city of Nazareth, into Judaea unto the city of David, which is called Bethlehem;(because he was of the house and lineage of David.) To be taxed with Mary his espoused wife, being great with child. And so, it was that while they were there the days were accomplished that she should be delivered. There, Mary brought forth her firstborn son and wrapped him in swaddling clothes and laid him in the Manger. For you see there was no room for them in the Inn."

Hebrews 12:14 NIV – "Make every effort to live in peace with everyone and be holy; without holiness, no one will see the Lord."

Galatians 5:22 NIV – "The fruit of the Spirit is Love, Joy, PEACE, Longsuffering, Kindness, Goodness, Faithfulness have its perfect work in you."

1 Peter 5:7 NIV – "Cast all your anxiety on him because he cares for you."

1 Thessalonians 5:15 NIV – "Make sure that nobody pays back wrong for wrong, but always strive to do what is good for each other and for everyone else."

Colossians 3:15 NIV – "Let the peace of Christ rule in your hearts, since as members of one body (family) you were called to peace. And be thankful."

Ephesians 3:17-19 KJV – "That Christ may dwell in your hearts through faith. I pray that you are being rooted and grounded in love, may have power together with all the saints to comprehend the length and height and depth of His Love. To know the love of Christ that surpasses knowledge, that you may be filled with all the fullness of God."

Colossians 3:16(a) NIV – "Let the love of Christ dwell in you richly."

2 Corinthians 10:3-5 NIV – "For though we Live in the world, we do not wage war as the world does. The weapons we fight with are not the weapons of the world. On the contrary, they have divine power to demolish strongholds. We demolish arguments and every pretension that sets itself up against the knowledge of God, and we take captive every thought to make it obedient to Christ."

Psalm 27:2 NIV – "When the wicked advance against me to devour me, it is my enemies and my foes who will stumble and fall."

Proverbs 3:5-8 KJV – "Trust in the LORD with all thine heart and lean NOT unto thine own understanding. In all thine ways acknowledge him, and he shall direct thy paths. Be NOT wise in thine own eyes: Fear the Lord and depart from evil. It shall be health to thy navel and marrow to thy bones."

Job 22:28 NIV – "You will also declare a thing, and it will be established for you; So, light will shine on your ways."

Deuteronomy 31:6 NIV – "Be strong and courageous. Do not be afraid or terrified because of them, for the LORD your God goes with you; he will never leave you nor forsake you."

Isaiah 41:10 NIV – "Fear not, for I am with you; do not be dismayed, for I am your God. I will strengthen you and help you; I will uphold you with my righteous right hand."

Ephesians 3:20 NASB – "To him who is able to do far more abundantly beyond all that we ask or think, according to the power that works within us."

Psalm 37:1-5 NKJV – "Fret not thyself because of evildoers, neither be thou envious against the workers of iniquity. For they shall soon be cut down like the grass, and wither as the green herb. Trust in the Lord, and do good; so shalt thou dwell in the land, and verily thou shalt be fed. Delight thyself also in the Lord: and he shall give thee the desires of thine heart. Commit thy way unto the Lord; trust also in him; and he shall bring it to pass."

Philippians 4:7 NIV – "And the peace of God which transcends all understanding and will guard your hearts and your minds in Christ Jesus."

Psalm 63:1-4 KJV – "O God, thou art my God; early will i seek thee: my soul thirst for thee, my flesh longeth for thee in a dry and thirsty land, where no water is; To see thy power and thy glory, so as I have seen thee in the sanctuary. Because thy lovingkindness is better than life, my lips shall praise thee. Thus, will I bless the while I live: I will lift up my hands in thy name."

Isaiah 26:3 KJV – "You will keep in perfect peace him whose mind is steadfast, because he trusts in you."

Psalm 88:13 CSB – "But I call to you for help, Lord in the morning my prayer meets you."